EXPLORING
CAREERS

Careers in the Legal Profession

ReferencePoint
Press®

Other titles in the *Exploring Careers* series include:

Careers in Food and Agriculture
Careers in Renewable Energy
Careers in Travel and Hospitality

Careers in the Legal Profession

Carla Mooney

ReferencePoint
Press®

© 2018 ReferencePoint Press, Inc.
Printed in the United States

For more information, contact:
ReferencePoint Press, Inc.
PO Box 27779
San Diego, CA 92198
www.ReferencePointPress.com

Picture credits:
 8: Maury Aaseng
13: iStockphoto.com/ferrantraite
20: Shutterstock.com/Creativa Images
50: Shutterstock.com/Dragon Images
58: iStockphoto/Image Source

LIBRARY OF CONGRESS CATALOGING-IN-PUBLICATION DATA

Name: Mooney, Carla, 1970– author.
Title: Careers in the Legal Profession/by Carla Mooney.
Description: San Diego, CA: ReferencePoint Press, Inc., 2018. | Series: Exploring Careers series | Includes bibliographical references and index. Identifiers: LCCN 2017040655 (print) | LCCN 2017040826 (ebook) | ISBN 9781682823149 (ebook) | ISBN 9781682823132 (hardback)
Subjects: LCSH: Law—Vocational guidance—United States—Juvenile literature.
Classification: LCC KF297 (ebook) | LCC KF297 .M659 2018 (print) | DDC 340.023/73—dc23
LC record available at https://lccn.loc.gov/2017040655

Contents

Working in the Legal Profession

Yolanda Lewis works in the legal profession in a job that the average person has probably never even heard of. Lewis is a court administrator for the Superior Court of Fulton County, Georgia. And although most people do not know what a court administrator is, her job is essential for the functioning of the court. Administrators like Lewis, in courthouses all across the United States, handle the managerial duties and administrative functions of a court system. Court administrators work in all types of courts. Their responsibilities include hiring and training new employees, maintaining the court's budget, and making sure all proceedings run smoothly. Court administrators also supervise courtroom employees and make sure each is performing his or her duties correctly. They organize court records and manage the flow of cases so that the court does not get behind schedule.

Every day, Lewis supervises nearly three hundred employees in one of Georgia's busiest and largest courts. She also supports twenty elected judges, oversees fifteen justice programs, and manages a budget of $24.5 million. Each day brings new challenges, but Lewis enjoys her work keeping the court running smoothly. Lewis said in a December 2016 article posted on the University of South Alabama website:

> One of my goals is to have a well-run court system for the judges and the citizens of Fulton County. I grew up in a small town with hard-working parents and grandparents. I do my best to be dedicated and prepared every day. That's how I learned to have a great work ethic. Leadership is about taking steps in the direction of our dream trusting that your passion will create new possibilities.

After earning a bachelor's degree in political science and criminal justice and a master's degree in public administration, Lewis has worked for sixteen years in court and public administration positions. Like many others working in the legal profession, Lewis strives to make sure the court serves the needs of the people of her community. "I have also worked with my staff to create a new court to serve our veterans who suffer from post-traumatic stress disorder, other brain injuries, and mental illness. I was able to write and secure a grant to fund the Veterans Court," she said. "We have also implemented the Video Remote Interpreting Technology Program to help citizens who have a language barrier."

Much More than Lawyers

When most people consider a career in law, they think of lawyers. However, the legal profession is a wide career field that includes many opportunities that do not require a time-consuming, expensive law degree. New regulations, advances in technology, and the increasing caseload in courts across the country are driving the demand for a growing number of legal professionals. Legal professionals work for law firms, courts, government agencies, consulting firms, and corporations in industries ranging from finance to health care. Regardless of industry or job function, legal professionals help people and organizations navigate the increasingly complex legal system.

While some legal professionals are lawyers, others work as paralegals, mediators, court interpreters, jury consultants, and compliance specialists. Some specialize in certain areas of law, such as criminal law, family law, or business law.

Demand for Legal Professionals

According to the Bureau of Labor Statistics, the demand for legal professionals is expected to grow at approximately 5 percent through 2024. One career in high demand is in e-discovery. In every legal case—whether civil or criminal—the parties are permitted to see each other's records and evidence. As in most other career fields, the

Careers in the Legal Profession

Occupation	Minimal Education Requirements	2016 Median Pay
Administrative assistant and secretary	High school diploma or equivalent	$37,230
Correctional officer and bailiff	High school diploma or equivalent	$42,820
Court interpreter	Bachelor's degree	$46,120
Court reporter	Postsecondary non-degree award	$51,320
Forensic science technician	Bachelor's degree	$56,750
Judge and hearing officer	Doctoral or professional degree	$109,940
Jury consultant	Bachelor's degree	$44,000
Lawyer	Doctoral or professional degree	$118,160
Private detective and investigator	High school diploma or equivalent	$48,190
Social worker	Bachelor's degree	$46,890

Source: Bureau of Labor Statistics, *Occupational Outlook Handbook*, 2015. www.bls.gov.

legal profession relies heavily on electronic preservation and transmission of these documents. E-discovery professionals help identify, preserve, collect, process, review, and produce electronic information that pertains to legal cases. To do this work, e-discovery professionals must be well versed in the use of technology and a variety of software programs. As important members of the legal team, they also need to have an understanding of laws and legal practices. As technology advances, e-discovery professionals are expected to become an even more important part of the legal process.

Across the legal profession, education requirements vary by career. While some legal careers require just a high school diploma or its equivalent, others require a bachelor's or master's degree from a four-year college or university or a juris doctor, or JD, degree from a law school. Students can major in a variety of fields depending on their interest, including paralegal studies, communication, political science, public administration, business, and economics. They study foundational classes in humanities, math, and English to strengthen their reading, writing, research, and communication skills. Often, students also take a wide variety of core legal classes, such as legal research, legal writing, contracts, property law, and more. In addition, many students concentrate in specific areas of the law, such as criminal, business, family, immigration, intellectual property, tax, environmental, and litigation. Across all positions, the preparation needed for a career as a legal professional can provide a foundation of skills that can be used in a wide range of careers.

Lawyer

On television, lawyers star in courtroom dramas where they spend most of their time in a packed courtroom arguing high-profile criminal cases in front of a judge and jury. While some lawyers do make impassioned arguments to juries to prosecute or defend criminals, many lawyers handle a variety of other legal needs, from wills and divorces to taxes and immigration.

Every day, lawyers advise their clients on a wide variety of legal issues. Depending on the lawyer and his or her type of practice, clients could be individuals, businesses, nonprofit groups, or government agencies. Lawyers research issues and interpret relevant laws, judicial rulings, and regulations so that they can advise clients about their legal rights and obligations. Lawyers also present evidence and argue on behalf of their clients in courts, before government agencies, and in private legal matters. In addition, lawyers spend long hours preparing and filing a multitude of legal documents, including lawsuits, appeals, wills, contracts, and deeds.

At a Glance

Lawyer

Minimum Educational Requirements
Doctoral or professional law degree

Personal Qualities
Solid analytical, problem-solving, communications, and research skills

Certification and Licensing
Must pass a state's written bar exam

Working Conditions
Office environment, some courtroom appearances

Salary Range
Median pay of $118,160 in 2016

Number of Jobs
As of 2014, about 778,700

Future Job Outlook
Projected growth of 6 percent through 2024

Many lawyers concentrate in a particular area of the law, such as criminal law, tax law, family law, environmental law, securities law, and litigation. Criminal lawyers represent the prosecution or the defense and present evidence and arguments at trial that support their client's position. Tax lawyers help clients understand and follow complicated tax regulations and pay the appropriate taxes on income, profits, and property. For example, they may advise a business how much tax it needs to pay for sales in different states. Family lawyers handle legal matters that affect families, such as divorce, child custody agreements, and adoptions. Environmental lawyers work on matters involving environmental laws and regulations. This might mean helping waste disposal companies ensure that their business practices and procedures meet all laws and regulations. Securities lawyers advise clients on legal issues related to the buying and selling of stocks. Litigation lawyers concentrate in lawsuits and disputes between two or more parties. These disputes can involve contracts, personal injuries, or property.

Christina Kirk is the managing partner of Kirk Law Group in Oklahoma City. She concentrates in family law, business law, and laws that deal with special education. "A lot of my work has to do with family drama—divorces, child custody, guardianships, family member adoptions, etc.," Kirk said in a September 2015 interview published on the Business News Daily website. One of the most rewarding parts of her job is being able to help others. "I am proud to help families that truly need it. To assist a grandmother that has reared her grandchild for several years finally get legal guardianship is rewarding. Walking out of a special education meeting with a family knowing that my presence was able to secure much needed valuable services for their child is indescribable," said Kirk.

How Do You Become a Lawyer?

Education

Becoming a lawyer takes several years of full-time schooling. To start, students who want to become lawyers must earn a bachelor's degree from a four-year college or university. Because there is no recommended course of study for pre-law, students can major in a variety of areas from political science to math. Common undergraduate majors include English, political science, history, business, journalism, and philosophy. In addition, courses in public speaking, government, history, economics, and mathematics are helpful for pre-law students.

Almost all law schools require prospective students to take the Law School Admission Test, or LSAT. This standardized test measures skills in reading comprehension, information management, analysis and critical thinking, reasoning, and argumentation, all skills that are important in a legal career.

Next, students must complete three years of study at a law school accredited by the American Bar Association (ABA) and earn a juris doctor, or JD, degree. At law school, students take classes on constitutional law, contracts, property law, civil procedure, and legal writing. Some law students choose to take classes in tax, labor, and corporate law.

Certification and Licensing

To practice law in any state, a lawyer must be admitted to the state's bar, an association that represents the practicing lawyers in a state. The requirements for admission vary by state, but most states require applicants to pass one or more licensing exams called bar exams, in addition to graduating from an ABA-accredited law school. Bar exams are intense two-day exams. Some state exams are so difficult that it is common for people to have to take them more than once before they pass. According to the National Conference of Bar Examiners, only 58 percent of people who took the exams in 2016 passed.

Lawyers who want to practice in multiple states generally have to take the bar exam in each state where they plan to practice. Some states have reciprocal agreements with other states that allow lawyers to practice in both states without having to sit for another full bar exam.

After being admitted to the bar, lawyers must keep up-to-date on current developments in the law and legal practice. Most states require lawyers to complete several hours of continuing legal education every two to three years. Many law schools and state or local bar associations provide continuing education courses to keep lawyers current on legal issues such as ethics, taxes, and health care.

Volunteer Work and Internships

Students interested in becoming lawyers can gain valuable experience by working in part-time jobs or summer internships in law firms, government agencies, and corporate legal departments. Some organizations may hire law students who have completed their first year of law school as summer associate interns. Summer internships at larger law firms are generally filled by students who have completed their second year of law school. Working as an intern can give students an idea of what type of law they would like to practice as well as help them make professional contacts that may lead to a full-time job in the future.

In addition, students interested in becoming a lawyer can participate in mock trial competitions and debate clubs or volunteer with local public interest organizations. In this way they can learn valuable skills that will help them stand out to potential employers.

A lawyer discusses a legal matter with his clients. Some lawyers litigate criminal or civil cases in court, but many work outside of courtrooms advising clients on legal matters involving taxes, child custody, estate planning, and many other issues.

Skills and Personality

Successful lawyers need solid analytical and problem-solving skills. To help clients solve legal problems, lawyers must analyze large amounts of information, determine what facts are relevant to a client's situation, and develop a viable solution. At the same time, they must be able to separate their personal feelings and emotions from the case in order to objectively evaluate the situation and effectively represent their clients. Because legal issues often require a significant amount of research, lawyers also need to have strong research skills and be able to find the applicable laws, regulations, and cases that apply to a client's matter.

In their job, lawyers communicate with many people, from clients and coworkers to judges and opposing counsel. Therefore, a lawyer must have strong communication skills. "Communication is without a doubt the corporate lawyer's most important skill: communication with the client, with the other side, with one's law firm partners and associates," says corporate lawyer Andrea Masters in an article posted on Law Crossing. This includes the ability to speak clearly, listen to others, and write effectively. Lawyers must be able to clearly present and explain their client's case to juries, judges, arbitrators, and opposing parties. They prepare many written documents such as wills, trusts, and powers of attorney that need to be written in precise language. In addition, lawyers must be able to establish trust so clients feel comfortable sharing personal details related to their case.

On the Job

Employers

Many lawyers work for law firms that represent clients in a variety of industries, from health care to manufacturing. Other lawyers work directly for companies or for federal, state, or local government agencies. Some lawyers have their own law practice. According to the Bureau of Labor Statistics (BLS), there were approximately 778,700 lawyers working in the United States in 2014. The areas of highest employment for lawyers in 2014 were law firms (48 percent), local governments (7 percent), state governments (5 percent), the federal government (5 percent), and finance and insurance (3 percent).

Working Conditions

Regardless of employer or industry, lawyers spend most of their time working in an office. Some travel to meet with clients in homes, hospitals, or prisons. Some lawyers travel to appear in court. Most work at least full time, with many working more than the typical forty hours per week. During trials or when trying to meet deadlines, lawyers often face pressure and work long hours, including nights and weekends. Lawyers who work in large law firms or in private practice often log additional hours researching legal issues and preparing and reviewing documents.

Earnings

According to the BLS, as of 2016 the median annual earnings for lawyers was $118,160. Salaries for lawyers can vary widely, based on their employer's size, type, and location. As of 2016, the lowest-paid 10 percent earned less than $56,910 a year, while the highest-paid 10 percent earned more than $208,000 annually. Experienced lawyers who are partners in large law firms generally earn more than less experienced lawyers or lawyers with their own practice.

Opportunities for Advancement

New lawyers are usually hired as associates and work under the supervision of more experienced lawyers. After several years, some lawyers advance to become partners of their law firms, which makes them partial owners of the firm. Other lawyers take jobs as in-house lawyers in a large company's legal department. Some lawyers choose to open their own law firm after gaining a few years of experience. A few experienced lawyers are elected or appointed to become judges, while others take jobs as law school professors and administrators.

What Is the Future Outlook for Lawyers?

According to the BLS's *Occupational Outlook Handbook*, jobs for lawyers are projected to increase 6 percent through 2024. This growth is being driven by an increasing need for legal services for individuals, businesses, and government agencies. While law firms are still expected to be the largest employers of lawyers, many large companies are projected to hire more in-house lawyers to cut costs related to hiring outside legal counsel. This will lead to an increase in jobs for lawyers in a variety of industries such as finance companies, consulting firms, and health care providers. In addition, all levels of government will continue to need lawyers to prosecute or defend civil and criminal cases. Job growth in government law jobs, however, may be slowed by budget restrictions.

Price competition among law firms may lead to some firms cutting costs by assigning work that was previously performed by lawyers to less expensive paralegals. This may slow some hiring growth in these firms. Overall though, job prospects for lawyers are expected to be good. As the number of students graduating from law school increases, competition for open positions will be strong. Therefore, candidates who are willing to relocate and have related work experience will have the best prospects for landing a job in the field.

Find Out More

American Association for Justice (AAJ)
777 Sixth St. NW, Suite 200
Washington, DC 20001
website: www.justice.org

The AAJ is a professional organization that provides trial attorneys with information and other resources to effectively represent clients. Its site has the latest news, information, and education opportunities for those interested in trial law.

American Bar Association (ABA)
321 N. Clark St.
Chicago, IL 60654
website: www.americanbar.org

The ABA is a voluntary bar association for lawyers and law students. Its site has resources and information for those interested in legal careers.

Association of Corporate Counsel (ACC)
1025 Connecticut Ave. NW, Suite 200
Washington, DC 20036

The ACC is a global bar association for in-house counsel who work for corporations, associations, and other organizations. Its site provides information about current issues, education, networking opportunities, and advocacy initiatives.

Paralegal

What Does a Paralegal Do?

Every lawyer needs a right-hand man or woman. Paralegals assist lawyers in almost every aspect of the latters' job, from drafting contracts to taking notes at trial. Paralegals help lawyers prepare for meetings, hearings, and trials by conducting legal research, drafting documents, and maintaining and organizing files. They investigate and gather facts for a client's case and arrange legal documents and evidence for lawyers to review as they prepare a case. Paralegals also schedule meetings and interviews with clients, witnesses, and others. They take affidavits and other formal statements that may be used in court. While in court, paralegals assist lawyers by handling exhibits, reviewing transcripts, and taking notes.

Paralegals use technology and computers to organize and maintain the mountain of documents generated for cases, often in an electronic filing system. They also conduct e-discovery, which is the process of identifying, collecting, and producing electronically stored information in response to a request related to a lawsuit or investigation. Electronically stored information includes e-mails, documents,

At a Glance

Paralegal

Minimum Educational Requirements
Associate's degree

Personal Qualities
Detail oriented, organized, efficient

Certification and Licensing
Not required, but can strengthen résumé

Working Conditions
Office environment, some courtroom appearances

Salary Range
Median pay of $49,500 in 2016

Number of Jobs
As of 2014, about 279,500

Future Job Outlook
Projected growth of 8 percent through 2024

presentations, databases, voice mail, audio and video files, social media, and websites.

Like lawyers, paralegals can concentrate in certain areas of the law, such as criminal, corporate, family, and immigration law. Criminal law or litigation paralegals primarily maintain client documents, conduct research related to a case, draft settlement agreements, and organize evidence and documents for depositions or trials. Some criminal law paralegals may also assist at trial or coordinate trial logistics such as reserving office space, transporting documents to court, and setting up computers and other equipment needed during the trial. Corporate paralegals often work on preparing many types of legal documents used in business, such as employee contracts, shareholder agreements, stock-option plans, and annual financial reports. They may also be involved in reviewing any government regulations that affect a business and making sure the company is in compliance.

Jamie Collins is a litigation paralegal in Indiana who concentrates in personal injury cases. Her favorite part of the job is preparing for a jury trial. In an interview posted on the Criminal Justice Degree Schools website, she says:

> While it can be exhausting to prepare for a jury trial, it is also very fulfilling and exhilarating. When you prepare for a trial, the case has a way of consuming you. You find yourself going without lunch, without dinner, without sleep because you become so immersed in the work or deep in thought about the case. . . . It is very inspiring to know that you are playing a vital role to help prepare a client's case for trial, their one day in court and one ultimate outcome. It feels great to know that you and your team gave the client everything you had to help them reach a final outcome.

How Do You Become a Paralegal?

Education

There are several ways a person can become a paralegal. Some paralegals earn an associate's degree in paralegal studies at a community college. In most paralegal studies programs, students take courses in legal research, legal writing, and legal computer applications. They also study areas of the law, such as corporate law and international law. Many paralegals earn a bachelor's degree in business, political science, fine arts, or any number of other subject areas. Regardless of their degree, students should have a foundation of classes in humanities and math, to have strengthened their reading, writing, and communication skills.

For people who earn a bachelor's degree in another field, a paralegal certificate program can provide the necessary training for a paralegal career. These programs provide intensive training in subjects such as legal research, legal writing, and various areas of the law. Most certificate programs require eighteen to forty-five credit hours and are often able to be completed at night, on weekends, or online if students are working in a full-time job. Most programs can be completed within a year.

A paralegal prepares documents for a court case. Paralegals assist lawyers in almost every aspect of their work; their duties include drafting contracts, helping with legal research, and interviewing clients and witnesses.

Certification and Licensing

Although not required, some paralegals choose to obtain certification. Several paralegal organizations offer paralegal certification, including the National Federation of Paralegal Associations (NFPA) and the National Association of Legal Assistants. Some states also offer paralegal certification. These programs may be administered by the state's bar association or the state's paralegal professional organization.

To earn a certification, students typically take an exam that assesses their skills and knowledge. For example, the NFPA offers a Paralegal Core Competencies exam. In addition, students must meet certain educational and/or work experience requirements to be certified. To keep their national certification current, paralegals must complete several hours of continuing legal education.

Some paralegals choose to earn advanced certifications such as the NFPA's Paralegal Advanced Competency Exam and become Registered Paralegals. To earn this certification, candidates must meet certain educational and work experience requirements, as well as pass an exam. Other paralegals choose to earn advanced certifications in certain specialties.

In some cases employers will hire candidates who do not have a degree or certificate in paralegal studies but have a college degree and experience in a related field such as tax preparation or criminal justice. However, those who get a degree and earn a certification are more likely to stand out to employers. "In a competitive job market, candidates can set themselves apart by becoming credentialed after completing their formal education," said Tracey Young, former president of the NFPA, in an article posted on the *U.S. News & World Report* website. "By successfully passing a voluntary certification exam such as the Paralegal CORE Competency Exam, candidates demonstrate their knowledge and understanding of the essential skills and concepts necessary to effectively work as a paralegal."

Internships

Students interested in becoming paralegals can gain valuable experience by working in part-time jobs or summer internships. Many paralegal studies programs offer students the opportunity to work in an internship, where they can gain practical work experience. Students can also intern with private law firms, public defenders, corporate legal departments, legal aid organizations, or government agencies. Working as an intern can give students an idea of what type of law they are interested in as well as help them develop technical skills and make professional contacts that may lead to a full-time job in the future.

Jessica Sebeck Lugo worked as a paralegal intern at the 3M Office of General Counsel. In her internship, Lugo reviewed contracts, researched international law, and provided litigation support for several paralegals and attorneys. "I couldn't have asked for a better internship experience. The support from my supervisor, the other staff, the department as a whole was incredible," said Lugo in an article posted on the website for Inver Hills Community College in Minnesota. The experience prepared her well, she says, for a future job in a corporate legal office.

Skills and Personality

To succeed on the job, paralegals must be highly organized and detail oriented, with strong computer and communication skills. Litigation and legal work create enormous quantities of documents and data. Lawyers depend on paralegals to organize and maintain all of this information and to access it quickly when needed—which means that paralegals must have strong computer skills and be familiar with a variety of database and software programs.

While lawyers are working on the big picture of the case, the smaller details often fall on paralegals to handle. Paralegals check documents for accuracy, manage the logistics of a court trial, track court dates and filing deadlines, and much more. Lawyer and professor Kirk Olson said in a November 2016 article on the website of Rasmussen College:

> Lawyers hire paralegals because a good paralegal will find flaws in documents and assist with billing and other detailed functions that keep a law office working. A good paralegal is a "deadline cop" who keeps the

law firm on track. . . . Finding and warning of a dead-line that others missed may prevent a loss of a client's case and may save a $10,000 deductible in a lawyer's malpractice claim!

Great communication skills are a must for paralegals. In their job, paralegals communicate with many people, from lawyers, clients, and coworkers to opposing counsel and investigators. They should be able to speak clearly, listen to others, and write effectively. Paralegals prepare many written documents such as contracts, wills, trusts, and powers of attorney that need to be written in precise language. In addition, they need to present legal research to lawyers and clients.

On the Job

Employers

Many paralegals work for law firms. Other paralegals work directly for companies or for federal, state, or local government agencies. According to the Bureau of Labor Statistics (BLS), there were approximately 279,500 paralegals working in the United States in 2014. The industries that employed the most paralegals in 2014 were law firms (72 percent), local governments (6 percent), the federal government (5 percent), state governments (4 percent), and finance and insurance (3 percent).

Working Conditions

Regardless of employer or industry, paralegals spend most of their time working in an office. Some travel to collect documents and information, attend depositions or court trials with lawyers, and other tasks. Often, paralegals must juggle multiple projects under tight deadlines. Most work full time, with some working more than forty hours per week when a deadline approaches.

Earnings

According to the BLS, as of May 2016 the median annual earnings for paralegals was $49,500. Salaries for paralegals can vary based on their employer's size, type, and location. As of May 2016, the lowest-paid 10 percent earned less than $31,070, while the highest-paid 10 percent earned more than $80,260.

Opportunities for Advancement

New paralegals usually work under the supervision of lawyers and more experienced paralegals. With experience, paralegals take on more complicated assignments. They may also become a supervisor, overseeing a project and a team of paralegals. Some paralegals choose to go to law school and become lawyers.

What Is the Future Outlook for Paralegals?

According to the BLS's *Occupational Outlook Handbook*, jobs for paralegals are projected to increase 8 percent through 2024. As law firms attempt to reduce costs, they are shifting some work from lawyers to less expensive paralegals. This includes some of the work traditionally done by entry-level lawyers, such as time-consuming document review. This is expected to increase demand for paralegals.

Although law firms are expected to remain the largest employer of paralegals, opportunities with in-house legal departments of large corporations are also expected to increase. Many large corporations are projected to hire more in-house lawyers and legal staff to cut costs related to hiring outside legal counsel. This will lead to an increase in jobs for paralegals in a variety of industries such as finance companies, consulting firms, and health care providers.

In times of slow economic growth, law firms may experience a slowdown in work, as fewer clients are involved in litigation, mergers, or other legal actions. In a slowdown, there will be less work for paralegals, which may limit growth in this career.

Overall, job prospects for paralegals are expected to be good. Because of the attractive salary and work environment, competition for open positions will be strong. Therefore, candidates who have a paralegal degree and/or certification, related work experience, and strong computer and database-management skills will have the best prospects for landing a job in the field.

Find Out More

American Bar Association (ABA)
321 N. Clark St.
Chicago, IL 60654
website: www.americanbar.org

Not just for lawyers, the ABA is a voluntary bar association also for paralegals and law students. Its site has resources and information for those interested in legal careers.

National Association of Legal Assistants (NALA)
7666 E. Sixty-First St., Suite 315
Tulsa, OK 74133
website: www.nala.org

NALA is a paralegal professional organization that provides a voluntary certification program, continuing legal education, and professional development programs for all paralegals.

National Federation of Paralegal Associations (NFPA)
One Parkview Plaza, Suite 800
Oakbrook Terrace, IL 60181
website: www.paralegals.org

The NFPA is a professional organization that promotes the paralegal profession globally. Its site has the latest news, information, and certification and education opportunities for those interested in a paralegal career.

National Paralegal Association (NPA)
PO Box 406
Solebury, PA 18963
website: www.nationalparalegal.org

The NPA is a professional organization that focuses on education for paralegals, offers a career guide, and provides a school directory. Membership includes a variety of levels, including students who are just beginning paralegal school.

Court Interpreter

What Does a Court Interpreter Do?

A record 64.7 million US residents, both foreign born and native born, spoke a language other than English at home in 2015, according to a report by the Center for Immigration Studies. Many of these residents have limited English skills, which becomes a challenge if and when they must deal with a legal matter.

Court interpreters work with judges and lawyers to help people who are not able to or are reluctant to communicate in English. Court interpreters work in various situations, such as meetings between clients and lawyers, depositions, court hearings, arraignments, and trials. Fluent in English and at least one other foreign language, they translate what is being said for clients and then translate their clients' responses back to the other participants. In addition to translating spoken conversations and testimony, court interpreters may also read and translate written documents and files. Some interpreters even work in sign language to help people who are hearing

At a Glance

Court Interpreter

Minimum Educational Requirements
Bachelor's degree recommended

Personal Qualities
Strong communication, interpersonal, and communication skills; cultural sensitivity

Certification and Licensing
Required for some states and courts

Working Conditions
Courtroom, office environment

Salary Range
Median pay of $46,120 in 2016*

Number of Jobs
As of 2014, about 61,000*

Future Job Outlook
Projected growth of 29 percent through 2024*

*Stats are for interpreters and translators, which includes court interpreters.

impaired or deaf. In addition, court interpreters must also be able to understand legal terms and be able to convey them in other languages to non-English speakers.

Not only must interpreters translate spoken messages quickly, accurately, and clearly, they must also convey the style, tone, and emotion of the original speaker or writer. "Nuance is everything," said Dana Marks, a veteran judge in San Francisco and president of the National Association of Immigration Judges, in a June 2017 article in the *Los Angeles Times*. "If things are said in different ways at different times, that can be an interpreter's fault, and yet, it makes the person look not credible."

Lesley Walker works as a Spanish-language court interpreter for the Sacramento Superior Court in California. In her job, she works in a variety of settings and courts. Every day brings something new. Once Walker receives an assignment, she heads to the assigned courtroom or interpreter's office. In an April 2016 interview posted on the Middlebury Institute of International Studies at Monterey website, Walker said, "From there, your day depends on what kind of hearing it is you are assigned to. An arraignment, continuance, or pretrial hearing may be very brief. A trial lasts all day every day for anywhere from a couple of days to several months. As a court interpreter, you will have to be available whenever you are needed, and this may require a lot of waiting around."

How Do You Become a Court Interpreter?

Education

The most important educational requirement for students interested in becoming a court interpreter is fluency in both reading and speaking English and at least one other language. In addition, most employers require interpreters to have a bachelor's degree from a four-year college or university. While many students earn a bachelor's degree in the foreign language they want to work with, others study subject areas that allow them to develop subject matter expertise. Some students earn a bachelor's degree in translation studies, concentrating on a foreign language and taking courses in diction, phonetics, composition, and translation processes.

Regardless of their major, students interested in becoming a court interpreter should take a variety of classes in English, writing, foreign languages, and computer science in order to develop skills that will be needed on the job. In addition, students may want to immerse themselves in a foreign culture in order to strengthen their language skills. To do this, they might travel to a foreign country or participate in a study abroad program. Speaking the language every day with native speakers improves students' abilities and teaches them the slang used in real life that might not be taught in a classroom. If travel is not an option, students can become involved with people who speak a foreign language in their community or read on a variety of subjects in both English and another language. Students interested in sign language interpreting may take classes in American Sign Language.

In addition to developing their reading, writing, and foreign language skills, students should also become familiar with legal terminology and concepts. Taking classes in various legal subjects can develop these necessary skills. Some students minor in judicial or law interpretation and translation, while others enroll in formal certificate programs.

Certification and Licensing

Certification requirements for court interpreters vary by court, state, and even language. Some state courts do not require certification and simply administer a language proficiency test for interpreters. Others require interpreters to be certified and administer oral and written certification tests. Some states have additional requirements for interpreters, such as attending classes and passing a background check. In federal courts, court interpreters for Spanish, Navajo, and Haitian Creole languages must become certified by completing the Federal Court Interpreter Certification Examination. Interpreters for other languages are qualified by the individual federal district courts.

Even if not required to be certified, some court interpreters choose to earn voluntary certifications to demonstrate proficiency in a foreign language and interpreting skills. The American Translators Association and the Translators and Interpreters Guild offer voluntary certifications in over twenty-five languages for court interpreters. For those interested in sign language interpreting, the National Association of the Deaf and the Registry of Interpreters for the Deaf jointly offer certification for general sign language interpreters. Students may also choose to enroll in a professional court interpreter certificate program, which will provide them with an understanding of US laws and the judicial system. These programs are offered by universities, community colleges, and professional organizations. Students study translating skills, court procedures, court interpreting, and the US penal code.

The test to become a certified court interpreter is very rigorous, regardless of language. These exams test language skills, legal vocabulary, and the ability to interpret simultaneously and not delay a court proceeding. "Just because someone speaks two languages does not mean they're going to be a good interpreter," said Polly Ryan, program coordinator of Minnesota's court interpreter program, in an article posted in January 2015 on the *Post Bulletin* website. "Sometimes people come in and are just so surprised when they bomb out on the test. They might be fluent, but it's a different skill set."

Volunteer Work and Internships

Many employers prefer interpreters with previous work experience. To gain valuable experience, students interested in becoming court interpreters can volunteer to interpret through community organizations and local sporting events that include international participants. Students may also volunteer or intern for a translation company to develop their skills. In some internships, students may work closely with a more experienced interpreter, particularly in industries with a high demand for interpreters, such as court and medical interpreting.

Working as a volunteer or an intern can help students build their language and interpreting skills and make professional contacts that may lead to a full-time job in the future. Anabella improved her interpreting skills by volunteering at small claims courts. "I was able to assist many litigants while continually improving my skills," she says in an interview posted on the California Courts website. Anabella also participated in the Superior Court of Orange County's Family Law Interpreter Internship Program. "Once a week for three months

I worked with pro bono attorneys, interpreted in pretrial conferences, and eventually interpreted before the judge, all while under supervision of a certified interpreter," she says.

Skills and Personality

Not every interpreter has the skills and personality to succeed in the courtroom. In addition to being fluent in both verbal and written language, court interpreters must have strong interpersonal skills and cultural sensitivity. In their job, they communicate with many people, including lawyers, clients, investigators, and judges. Court interpreters must be good listeners. Even when other activity is taking place around them, they must be able to focus on the individuals for whom they are translating, and they must accurately relay what is being said or asked. In addition, because some court testimony may be shocking or graphic, court interpreters must be able to keep their emotions in check and not express personal opinions or take a side when interpreting. "Legal interpreting requires great objectivity and detachment. The legal interpreter cannot improvise so as to facilitate communication. He or she must render directly the utterances produced by the legal actors," Piers Armstrong, director of the Spanish-English legal interpreting and translation certificate program at California State University–Los Angeles, says in a CBS interview.

The ability to stay calm in stressful situations is another essential element of being a court interpreter. People who are appearing in court are often agitated. The only way to accurately interpret their comments without losing meaning and tone is to remain calm and clear at all times.

On the Job

Employers

According to the Bureau of Labor Statistics (BLS), there were approximately sixty-one thousand interpreters (who work in spoken or sign language) and translators (who work in written language) working in 2014. This group includes court interpreters. The industries that employed the most interpreters and translators in 2014 were professional, scientific, and technical services (29 percent); educational services (26 percent); health care and social assistance (16 percent); and government (7 percent). In addition, one in five interpreters and translators were self-employed.

Working Conditions

Court interpreters work primarily in courtrooms and law offices, where they assist in client meetings, depositions, and various court proceedings. Most interpreters work full-time during regular business hours. Those who are self-employed may have more variable schedules, with varying workloads.

Earnings

According to the BLS, as of May 2016 the median annual earnings for interpreters and translators, which includes court interpreters, was $46,120. Salaries for interpreters and translators can vary according to languages, skill, experience, employer, certifications, and location. Interpreters with fluency in high-demand languages or languages with few qualified interpreters often earn higher salaries. As of May 2016, the lowest-paid 10 percent earned less than $25,370, while the highest-paid 10 percent earned more than $83,010.

Opportunities for Advancement

With experience, a court interpreter might take on more complicated assignments, such as a complex, multiday trial. Some interpreters choose to start their own business after they have established themselves in the industry. With good referrals from existing clients, they can get new work and establish new working relationships.

What Is the Future Outlook for Court Interpreters?

According to the BLS's *Occupational Outlook Handbook*, jobs for interpreters and translators are projected to increase 29 percent through 2024. This rate of growth is much faster than the average growth rate of all other occupations. Increasing globalization and a more diverse US population are the primary drivers of growth in this career. Projected increases in the number of Spanish-speaking residents in the United States are expected to fuel greater demand for Spanish-language interpreters. Strong demand is also expected for interpreters of French, German, Portuguese, Russian, and Arabic—among other languages.

Job prospects for court interpreters are good. Those candidates with at least a bachelor's degree and some professional certifications and/or a master's degree in oral interpreting or written translation will have the best opportunities. Candidates willing to move to urban areas such as New York, San Francisco, Los Angeles, and Washington, DC—areas with large immigrant populations—will find the largest numbers of available jobs.

Find Out More

American Translators Association (ATA)
225 Reinekers Lane, Suite 590
Alexandria, VA 22314
website: www.atanet.org

The ATA is a professional association for people in translation and interpreting professions. Its website offers information about careers, industry news and issues, certification, and more.

Interpreters Guild of America (IGA)
e-mail: info@interpretersguild.org
website: www.interpretersguild.org

The IGA is an organization created by and for independent interpreters and is committed to advocating for the profession. Its website offers job search resources for members as well as recent industry news.

National Association of Judiciary Interpreters & Translators (NAJIT)
2002 Summit Blvd., Suite 300
Atlanta, GA 30319
website: www.najit.org

The NAJIT promotes the highest professional standards in legal interpreting. Its website offers information about careers, industry news and issues, and events.

Mediator

Litigation is time consuming and costly for everyone involved. To reduce legal costs and avoid long, drawn-out legal proceedings, many people try to settle their disputes out of court. They do this with the help of a mediator. Mediators engage in a process known as alternative dispute resolution (ADR). In an effort to reduce court caseloads, some states have made it mandatory for litigants to take part in this process before they go to trial with a dispute. ADR allows litigants to explore and negotiate solutions with the assistance of a mediator. Mediators are neutral and do not represent or advocate for either party in a dispute. Instead, they attempt to bring the parties together so they can agree to a compromise. "Settling a dispute in court would have torn my family apart," said a past mediation participant in a May 2017 article posted on the Hartford County Living website. "Instead, three sessions of mediation guided us to a win-win resolution. I was very

At a Glance

Mediator

Minimum Educational Requirements
Bachelor's degree

Personal Qualities
Strong problem-solving and conflict-resolution skills, ability to remain calm and objective in emotional confrontations

Certification and Licensing
Required in some states

Working Conditions
Office environment

Salary Range
Median pay of $59,770 in 2016*

Number of Jobs
As of 2014, about 8,400*

Future Job Outlook
Projected growth of 9 percent through 2024*

*Stats are for mediators, arbitrators, and conciliators.

impressed with the mediators, and they didn't tell us what to do. Mediation saved us time, money, and, most importantly, it brought my family back together." If the mediation process fails, the case can still proceed to trial.

Mediators work on almost any type of civil case. They can become involved in class action lawsuits, when a number of people get together as a group to sue a company or organization. They mediate contract disputes between two or more companies. They can become involved in all types of commercial litigation, such as when one party sues another for breach of contract or when there are disputes between partners or shareholders of a business. Mediators also handle labor and employment disputes, such as when an employee sues a company for sexual harassment, discrimination, or wrongful termination. Some mediators focus on the family, working to settle disputes involving child custody agreements or equitable distribution of assets in a divorce.

Mediators' specific job duties vary by the court and state in which they work. In most cases, however, they conduct initial meetings with the parties to go over how the arbitration process will work. They set fees and clarify details such as number of witnesses and time requirements. They set up private, confidential meetings for parties, facilitate discussion between parties, and control the direction of negotiations. When a solution is agreed on, the mediator documents it and prepares court reports and settlement agreements.

Ellen Feldman is a mediator and partner at CEL & Associates, a firm that specializes in pre- and postdivorce mediation. Although she started her career as a lawyer, Feldman began working as a mediator after taking a break from the working world to raise her children. One of the best parts of her job, she says, is helping people resolve their disputes so that they can avoid the expense and emotional turmoil of court trials. "Mediation is a much better fit for my personality than commercial litigation. . . . I really love the fact that I mediate full-time and I am always looking for a way to solve a problem instead of the best way to advocate for a client's position without regard for the other side. I do not have trouble persuading people that mediation is better than litigating a divorce," she said in a September 2015 interview posted on the Next Act for Women website.

Other people interested in conflict resolution become arbitrators or conciliators. While arbitrators and conciliators are similar to mediators, there are some differences in these professions. Conciliators can propose a solution to end a conflict, while a mediator assists the parties in crafting their own solution. Often arbitrators work to resolve disputes as part of a multiperson panel that hears arguments from both parties in a dispute. The arbitration panel's decision is usually binding to both parties involved in the case. In contrast, mediators often work alone and to help both parties come up with a nonbinding, mutually agreeable compromise.

How Do You Become a Mediator?

Education

There is no single path to becoming a mediator. Many mediators have worked as lawyers or judges, although nonlawyers also work as mediators. Those who do not have a law degree usually at least have a bachelor's degree, often in subject areas such as criminal justice, legal studies, counseling, or social work. Some universities, such as Columbia University in New York City and the University of Massachusetts at Boston, offer master's degrees in mediation or conflict resolution. Students can also develop skills needed in this career by taking courses in social work, psychology, conflict resolution, marketing, public administration, and professional writing. Some positions require candidates to have a law degree, a master's in business administration, or other advanced degree.

Mediators who are appointed by the court to a case or are listed on the court's roster of mediators are typically required to meet training or experience standards. While these requirements vary by state and court, most states require court mediators to complete twenty to forty hours of basic mediation training. Training is offered by independent mediation programs, national and local mediation professional organizations, and postsecondary schools. "Mediation training involves education about the process, simulated mediation sessions, and critique by seasoned professionals," said mediator Ellen Feldman in a September 2015 interview posted on the Next Act for

Women website. Mediators who want to specialize in areas such as divorce and child custody, elder issues, and environmental disputes often need to take advanced training courses. In addition to training, some states also require new mediators to work with an experienced mediator for a certain number of cases. For mediators who work for community organizations, a basic mediation training course along with a bachelor's degree in a related field may be sufficient.

Certification and Licensing

Although there is no national license for mediators, some states require mediators to become certified to work on certain types of cases. This is true in Florida, for instance. Mediators who work in the state's county courts, circuit courts, and family courts must meet education requirements, complete a Florida Supreme Court–approved mediation certificate course in their specialty, observe or co-mediate several mediation cases in that specialty, and be found to have a good moral character. Because individual courts often have their own criteria to list a mediator on their court roster, it is recommended that a person who wants to mediate contact the court to learn the specific requirements.

Internships

Students interested in a career as a mediator can learn about this field by working in an internship for community and nonprofit organizations that provide mediation services. In this way students can observe community mediators in action to learn more about the profession. In an internship, students can also gain related work experience and develop skills that will help them stand out to potential employers.

While in college studying social work, Catie Eichberg worked for a semester as an intern for the Mediation Center, a nonprofit organization in Buncombe County, North Carolina. In the internship, Eichberg worked in the Community Mediation Program. The experience helped her learn about mediation and develop valuable skills. In an interview posted on the Mediation Center website, Eichberg says:

> I was able to gain a wealth of experience practicing my listening skills, and in conjunction with those, my communication skills, through my internship at The

Mediation Center. Conducting intake appointments and working one-on-one with clients provided me so many opportunities to fine-tune my listening skills, and that is something that will serve me well. . . . I also developed my documentation skills, which were essential to performing my responsibilities well.

Skills and Personality

Successful mediators have strong interpersonal skills, such as being able to work with people from all backgrounds while displaying a calm demeanor and sensitivity toward others. These skills are essential because mediators nearly always work with people who have strong—and often highly emotional—disagreements. They must be able to calmly sort through the issues with the parties, guiding them little by little toward a resolution. This also requires skills in problem solving, analysis, and conflict resolution. Mediators must carefully weigh the facts of the case and apply appropriate laws and rules. Demonstrating neutrality, honesty, and patience are also critical skills, since mediators must remain impartial and not favor one side over another during the mediation process.

Good communication is central to the work of any mediator. He or she must be a good listener because sometimes people are unclear about what they really want. Gaining an understanding of each side's position is not always easy, but it is important because without that, an agreement will be impossible to attain. Mediators must also be capable of communicating, verbally and in writing, with other professionals, including lawyers, judges, and others who might have an interest in the case.

On the Job

Employers and Working Conditions

Mediators work mainly for law firms, government agencies, courts, and community organizations that provide mediation services. According to the Bureau of Labor Statistics (BLS), there were approximately eighty-four hundred arbitrators, mediators, and conciliators in 2014. The industries that employed the most of these professionals in 2014 were legal services (19 percent); state governments and courts (15 percent); local governments and courts (15 percent); religious, grant-making, civic, professional, and other community organizations (5 percent); and finance and insurance (4 percent).

Earnings

According to the BLS, as of May 2016 the median annual earnings for the job category of mediators, arbitrators, and conciliators was $59,770. The lowest-paid 10 percent earned less than $32,550, while the highest-paid 10 percent earned more than $123,930. Generally, mediators employed by state government agencies and courts earned the highest salaries, with a median annual salary of $63,630 in May 2016.

Opportunities for Advancement

With experience, a mediator can take on more-complicated assignments. Some mediators start their own business after they have established themselves in the industry. With good referrals from existing clients, they can get new work and establish new working relationships. Earning voluntary professional certifications or an advanced degree in a related field can also improve a person's opportunities for advancement.

What Is the Future Outlook for Mediators?

According to the BLS's *Occupational Outlook Handbook*, mediator, arbitrator, and conciliator jobs are projected to increase 9 percent through 2024. However, because there are a relatively small number of jobs in this field, this growth is expected to create only about eight hundred new positions in the coming years.

As legal costs continue to skyrocket and court caseloads rise, ADR is becoming an increasingly popular alternative to lawsuits. As a result, opportunities for mediators are expected to increase. In addition, many contracts, such as employment or real estate contracts, are including clauses that require disputes to be decided through mediation or arbitration, which will increase the need for qualified mediators.

Because many mediators work for state or local governments, employment growth may be limited by budget restrictions. And in some situations, going to trial is preferred over out-of-court mediation.

Overall, job prospects for mediators are expected to be good. Candidates who have a law degree and have expertise in a variety of legal issues will have the best job prospects. In addition, lawyers with expertise in a particular area, such as environmental or corporate law, may have an advantage when applying for jobs in the field because they have an in-depth knowledge of complex issues and nuances that are specific to a particular type of case.

Find Out More

American Arbitration Association
120 Broadway, 21st Floor
New York, NY 10271
website: www.adr.org

The American Arbitration Association is an organization for people interested in arbitration and mediation careers. The website offers industry news and information as well as educational resources such as webinars, in-person programs, and on-demand courses.

American Mediation Association
3010 Lyndon B. Johnson Freeway, Suite 1200
Dallas, TX 75234
website: www.americanmediation.org

Formed in 1989, the American Mediation Association serves the legal and insurance communities and provides alternate dispute resolution through its panel of mediators and arbitrators.

Association for Conflict Resolution (ACR)
1639 Bradley Park Dr., Suite 500-142
Columbus, GA 31904
website: www.acrnet.org

The ACR is a professional organization dedicated to enhancing the practice and public awareness of conflict resolution. Its website has information about membership, chapters, education, and other resources of interest to current and prospective mediators.

National Association of Certified Mediators
244 Fifth Ave., Suite T-205
New York, NY 10001
website: www.mediatorcertification.org

The National Association of Certified Mediators offers a basic forty-hour mediator training course for people interested in this career. The website also has information on more advanced certification courses.

Compliance Officer

What Does a Compliance Officer Do?

Businesses today face an increasingly complicated maze of laws, regulations, licensing, and permits that impact their day-to-day operations. Compliance officers help their companies navigate the legal and regulatory minefield, making sure that they follow internal policies and regulatory requirements. Compliance officers ensure that employees follow rules and regulations and that no illegal or unethical behavior is occurring.

Compliance officers work in a broad range of industries, from health care to finance. Their responsibilities include conducting research on laws and regulations, evaluating the risks and regulations that affect an organization, setting up controls and procedures to mitigate these risks, and monitoring and reporting on how effective these controls and procedures are. They might also conduct staff training and prepare internal communications about possible areas of compliance risk. In an interview posted

At a Glance

Compliance Officer

Minimum Educational Requirements
Bachelor's degree recommended

Personal Qualities
Leadership skills, analytical and problem-solving skills, integrity, strong communication and interpersonal skills

Certification and Licensing
Voluntary

Working Conditions
Office environment

Salary Range
Median pay of $66,540 in 2016

Number of Jobs
As of 2016, about 273,910

Future Job Outlook
Projected growth of 3 percent through 2024

on the International Compliance Association website, Morven Grierson, compliance manager for a UK financial planning firm, says:

> Much of my time is spent monitoring the controls I have put in place to mitigate compliance risk. . . . I will use this information to identify any trends or new risks to the business and advise the Board on whether we need to take any remedial action. Remedial action can come in the form of amendments to policy and procedures and/or training and development of the firm's employees.

The focus of the compliance officer differs depending on the needs of the company and the industry. Contract compliance officers review contracts, policies, and procedures to ensure they follow applicable regulations. Trade compliance officers focus on import and export compliance issues. They ensure that a company's trade practices meet global trade regulations and that all required documentation is accurately prepared in a timely manner. Business compliance officers focus on developing and promoting a strong code of ethics within an organization. They identify and evaluate potential ethics and compliance risks and develop ways to minimize them. These officers also develop and implement codes of conduct and employee policies. Environmental compliance officers focus on environmental laws. They monitor organization activities such as waste management, noise pollution, and industrial hygiene procedures. If needed, they also obtain air and water permits and perform compliance audits. These officers work to create a safe and healthy working environment for employees.

Odell Guyton has worked as the chief compliance officer at Microsoft Corporation and is currently leading global compliance at Jabil Inc., an electronics manufacturer. According to Guyton, prevention is a huge part of a compliance officer's work. The goal of every compliance employee is to prevent a compliance breach before it occurs. Often, that involves educating managers and employees about compliance issues and potential pitfalls. In a *Wall Street Journal* article, Guyton asserts that much of his work involves what he calls "preventative law," or "helping [managers] to understand the business of the company, and helping them navigate around these land mines they may not be aware of in terms of compliance risk."

How Do You Become a Compliance Officer?

Education

There is no specific degree required for a career in compliance. Most entry-level compliance officers have a bachelor's degree from a four-year college or university. However, some employers prefer candidates with a master's degree in a field related to their industry, while other employers prefer candidates to have a law degree. Melissa Lea, the chief compliance officer for business-software maker SAP AG, believes that a legal background is useful but not always necessary for compliance careers. "What I look for personally is a passion for compliance and for training," she says in a *Wall Street Journal* article.

Specific education requirements for compliance positions vary by job, but many positions require some knowledge of the business and industry in which a compliance officer is employed. For example, compliance officers working in the finance industry often have a bachelor's degree in finance, economics, or a related field. Those working in the health care industry may be required to have a degree in a related health care field. Environmental compliance officers often have a degree in environmental science or a related field. Regardless of degree, students interested in compliance careers should take courses in management and leadership, writing, public speaking, communications, and ethics to build skills that are essential for this career. Once hired, many new compliance employees also receive on-the-job training.

Previous work experience in a prospective employer's industry is helpful. "Other past work experience could include internal audit, legal, human resources, internal controls and risk management," says Keith Darcy, executive director of the Ethics & Compliance Officers Association, in an article posted on the *U.S. News & World Report* website. "Prospective candidates should first learn how a job is defined and structured, including what issues it is responsible for. For example, a regulatory compliance officer must possess a different set of qualifications than an ethics and compliance officer."

Certification and Licensing

Although there are no required certifications for a compliance career, some employers prefer candidates to hold voluntary certifications in their industry. Several organizations offer compliance certifications for professionals working in specific industries. For example, the National Association of Federally-Insured Credit Unions (NAFCU) offers the NAFCU Certified Compliance Officer certification. Candidates earn the certification by passing an examination. The American Bankers Association offers the Certified Regulatory Compliance Manager certification. Candidates must pass an exam, obtain a professional recommendation, and meet certain experience requirements. In the health care industry, the Health Care Compliance Association offers several certifications. To earn one of these certifications, candidates must pass an exam and meet on-the-job experience requirements.

Internships

Students interested in this career path can learn more about a career in compliance by interning with a local company or shadowing someone who already works in the field. In this way they can gain related work experience and learn the skills that will help them stand out to potential employers. They may also make professional contacts in the industry that may help on a future job search.

While earning a bachelor's degree in environment, economy, development, and sustainability at Ohio State University, Taylor Faecher worked in a summer internship for Renergy Inc., a renewable energy company. In an interview on the university website, Faecher talks about his experience:

> I worked on OEPA [Ohio Environmental Protection Agency] reporting requirements, did a lot of data management for our beneficial reuse side of the business, and helped to secure additional funding through government programs, just to name a few tasks I was responsible for. The work was broad and informative. Being able to adapt, stay organized, and prioritize tasks were essential skills in the success of my internship.

Faecher was able to use his internship experience to get a full-time job with the company after his 2016 graduation. "Now I'm the Environmental Compliance Specialist with Renergy and am excited about what the future holds for this company!" he says.

Skills and Personality

Compliance officers must possess certain skills and qualities if they are to succeed in the career. "The most important skills include leadership, writing, public speaking, ethical decision-making, communications and training and instructional design," says Darcy. "They should also possess a high degree of courage and integrity due to the confidential nature of the work."

In addition, successful compliance officers have solid analytical and problem-solving skills. They spend much of their time gathering a wide range of information about laws and regulations. They must be able to analyze this information quickly if they are to propose policies and procedures and make useful recommendations. Because every company is different and must follow different rules and regulations, the analyst must be able to think creatively.

Compliance officers must have strong interpersonal skills and be able to communicate clearly to other company employees—both in person to person and in formal presentations. Because part of their job involves talking with employees and evaluating compliance with laws and regulations, they also need to have good listening skills.

On the Job

Employers and Working Conditions

According to the Bureau of Labor Statistics (BLS), there were approximately 273,910 compliance officers working in the United States in 2016. The industries that employed the most compliance officers in 2016 were the federal government (20 percent), state governments (13 percent), local governments (10 percent), and management of companies and enterprises (6 percent).

Compliance officers work in a variety of environments, from reviewing documents in an office to conducting compliance fieldwork in industrial factories or outdoors. For example, an environment compliance officer may spend a significant amount of time performing sophisticated tests outdoors to measure the environmental effects of a factory's chemical emissions. Most compliance officers work at least forty hours per week, with many putting in longer hours, which can include working on evenings and weekends when a deadline approaches.

Earnings

According to the BLS, as of May 2016 the median annual pay for compliance officers was $66,540. Salaries for compliance officers can vary according to experience and industry. As of May 2016, the lowest-paid 10 percent earned less than $37,630, while the highest-paid 10 percent earned more than $105,260.

Opportunities for Advancement

Experienced compliance officers usually get to take on more responsibility and work on complex projects. Senior officers may supervise teams of employees on a large project. Some compliance officers may advance to higher-level positions or even become a top executive in their firm, such as chief compliance officer.

Experienced compliance officers with a track record of excellent work are more likely to be considered for a promotion. In addition, those who have earned professional certifications or a master's degree in a field related to their industry or a law degree are also more likely to have more opportunities to advance. Jack Kelly, managing director of a compliance recruiting firm, says that building strong relationships with others in the business is also an important part of moving up the compliance career ladder. In an interview posted on the eFinancialCareers website, Kelly says:

> You're looking to show that you're proactive, doing things to make yourself more marketable and add value. Cultivate not just knowledge but also people skills, interpersonal skills. To rise in the ranks, you

have to have an understanding [of] how to work well and communicate effectively with businesspeople, senior executives, peers and underlings. Work on your holistic skill base and the personal side of who you are in a professional setting so people want to select you, promote you and move you forward.

What Is the Future Outlook for Compliance Officers?

According to the BLS, jobs for compliance officers are projected to increase 3 percent from 2014 to 2024, adding eighty-seven hundred new jobs. As government agencies such as the Consumer Financial Protection Bureau, the Financial Industry Regulatory Authority, and the US Environmental Protection Agency pass new regulations, compliance officers will be needed for organizations across many industries. "The regulatory environment in the U.S. is driving the hiring," says Paul McDonald, a senior executive director at human resources consulting firm Robert Half International, in a *Wall Street Journal* article. The outlook is "very bright for anyone entering into compliance as a career," he says. Those candidates with at least a bachelor's degree and some professional certifications and/or a master's degree in a field related to their industry will have the best opportunities.

Find Out More

Association of Insurance Compliance Professionals
11130 Sunrise Valley Dr., Suite 350
Reston, VA 20191
website: www.aicp.net

The Association of Insurance Compliance Professionals is an organization dedicated to serving and supporting the compliance professional in the insurance industry. Its website has information and resources, including a career center, local chapters, and events.

Ethics & Compliance Initiative (ECI)
2345 Crystal Dr., Suite 201
Arlington, VA 22202
website: www.ethics.org

With a history dating back to 1922, the ECI brings together ethics and compliance professionals and academics from all over the world to share techniques, research, and new ideas. The website includes information about research, job boards, industry news and issues, and certification.

National Society of Compliance Professionals
22 Kent Rd.
Cornwall Bridge, CT 06754
website: www.nscp.org

The National Society of Compliance Professionals is an organization dedicated to serving and supporting compliance professionals in the financial services industry. Its website has information and resources, including webinars, conferences, and more.

Litigation Support Professional

What Does a Litigation Support Professional Do?

The enormous amount of data and documents that the legal profession generates can be overwhelming. Litigation support professionals are an essential part of the legal team, using software and applications to keep all of these documents organized and easily accessible to legal staff. This career combines some of the legal skills and knowledge of lawyers and paralegals with the technical skills of information technology professionals.

Litigation support professionals identify, collect, and preserve information that is relevant to litigation. This includes e-mails, spreadsheets, voice mails, and other digital data. They design and implement databases to electronically manage, sort, index, abstract, and coordinate all of the litigation data. They are also responsible for developing data management strategies, providing user support and training on database and other

At a Glance

Litigation Support Professional

Minimum Educational Requirements
Bachelor's degree

Personal Qualities
Strong analytical, logical-thinking, and problem-solving skills; attention to detail

Certification and Licensing
Optional

Working Conditions
Office environment

Salary Range
Median pay of $83,855 in 2017

Future Job Outlook
Projected growth of 8 percent through 2022*

*Stats are for computer occupations in the legal industry, which includes litigation support professionals.

A litigation support professional reviews documents that he will need to organize and preserve for later use. Because they manage large amounts of data for legal cases, individuals who do this work must have some legal knowledge and exceptional IT skills.

data management software, and coordinating with technology vendors. During a trial, litigation support professionals may be a part of the courtroom legal team, assisting lawyers with technology in the courtroom.

Some individuals who work in this field develop areas of specialty. Document coders review and code documents, files, and other data so that the legal team can easily search and access information during a case. Litigation support analysts and specialists build and maintain databases for large, complex litigation, often designing systems to hold millions of documents. Project managers supervise teams of litigation support professionals on large-scale litigation projects.

Another area of litigation support is e-discovery. E-discovery professionals help produce, identify, preserve, collect, process, and review large quantities of electronic information that is exchanged between parties in both civil and criminal cases. Their work helps prevent loss, tampering, or damage of electronic evidence.

For many litigation support professionals, a main part of the job is setting up and maintaining a database that meets a legal team's needs and ensuring that it operates efficiently. They use specialized software to store and organize large amounts of information so it can be easily accessed and interpreted by authorized users. Once a database is established, litigation support professionals monitor its performance and modify it as needed. Because many legal databases hold sensitive information such as financial or personal data, securing that information is a priority.

Amy Bowser-Rollins is a litigation support manager who has worked in the field for more than seventeen years. When one of her law firm's clients, a large communications company, filed for bankruptcy, her firm handled the client's responses to ongoing information requests related to the bankruptcy proceedings. In an interview posted on the Paralegal 411 website, Bowser-Rollins says:

> We collected ESI (electronic stored information) from 126 custodians. In the end, we collected 12 terabytes, which equated to 148 billion e-mails with 38 billion attachments. Additionally, we scanned 2.8M pages of hardcopies and listened to recorded voicemails. With a case this size, designing an efficient workflow is key. I worked very closely with an excellent senior paralegal. She and I designed the workflow and maintained the workflow so that multiple offices of attorneys could assist.

Bowser-Rollins advises litigation support professionals to stay up-to-date on the latest technologies and trends.

How Do You Become a Litigation Support Professional?

Education

Most litigation support professionals have at least a bachelor's degree from a four-year college or university, often in computer science or information technology. Some of these professionals have both a law degree and a degree in information technology or computer science. In preparation for a job as a litigation support professional, course work in or experience with all sorts of databases is essential. "A huge part of the job is working with databases," says Bowser-Rollins in an article posted on the Litigation Support Guru website. "A basic knowledge of databases in general, regardless of the software, will go a long way. I am referring specifically to knowledge about database tables and fields, database records, data types and delimiters. I would also toss in there database queries, both full text boolean searches and fielded searches (or search by field)." Many litigation support professionals also attend industry trainings, seminars, and conferences where they learn new skills in document management systems, trial presentation software, hardware, and graphics applications.

In additional to technical skills, litigation support professionals must also have some knowledge of the legal system and the discovery process so that they can design a useful and efficient document work flow for the team. In many law firms, litigation support professionals either have law degrees or have worked in some capacity for a law firm. For example, June Huie, an information technology director for a Kansas law firm, says her experience working as a paralegal gave her a better understanding of how information technology and database systems are used in a law firm and how to make them more useful. "You can't just go buy any software. You have to have an idea of the business aspect of the firm," Huie says in an article posted on the Bureau of Labor Statistics (BLS) website.

Certification and Licensing

While not required, obtaining certifications can improve a person's chances of landing a job or getting promoted. Professional organizations such as the Organization of Legal Professionals offer litigation support and e-discovery certifications. To earn one, candidates must have a certain level of experience and pass an exam. Many candidates prepare for certification exams by studying on their own, doing an online course, and getting hands-on experience.

Internships

Students interested in this career can learn more about the field by doing an internship. Some students intern with law firms in litigation support or e-discovery roles, while others take database administration internships with other companies to get work experience and develop their technical skills. In the summer of 2016, Cameron Zell, a student at High Point University in North Carolina, worked as a digital forensics and professional services intern with RVM Enterprises. The company works with corporations and law firms to recover and manage electronic data. In the internship, Zell learned how to handle e-discovery and other data processing projects. "I provided assistance in guiding projects from beginning to end in order to help clients meet deadlines and achieve goals through the entire eDiscovery process," says Zell in an article posted on the High Point University website. "This part of my job included analyzing and processing data for large lawsuits and government inquiries."

Additionally, people interested in this career might want to shadow a professional in the field to learn more about the day-to-day job responsibilities. In an article posted on the Litigation Support Guru website, Bowser-Rollins recommends:

> I would suggest if they have a litigation support team where they work, ask them if they can shadow a litigation support professional while they're doing their work or attending meetings with attorneys. . . . Another suggestion would be for them to offer to work on litigation cases with eDiscovery to gain exposure to the databases, service providers and web-based review tools.

Skills and Personality

Successful litigation support professionals have solid organizational, analytical, and problem-solving skills. They need to make sense of all the data and information related to litigation and be able to organize it in a clear and meaningful way so it can be easily retrieved when needed. They must be able to monitor and analyze a database's performance and evaluate complex systems. Working with databases can be complex, and small errors can cause big problems. To prevent costly mistakes, litigation support professionals must be extremely detail oriented. Morgan Garcia-Lamarca has more than a decade of experience in e-discovery and litigation support. On the Relativity website, he explains:

> Troubleshooting is an everyday part of litigation support and a skill that requires both practice and a strong foundation of knowledge. Incoming data won't always be to specifications, workflows will not always produce the results expected, and whomever you are supporting will not always ask things you know how to answer—and that's okay. The difference between being good at your job and being great at your job is how you approach these situations.

Litigation support professionals must also have excellent communication skills. In their job, these professionals spend a lot of time interacting with people who do not have a technical background, such as lawyers, clients, and paralegals. Litigation support professionals must be able to explain technical concepts and how to use systems to nontechnical people.

On the Job

Employers and Working Conditions

Litigation support professionals primarily work for law firms, large corporations, and legal consulting firms. Regardless of employer, people working in litigation support spend most of their time working in an office. Some travel to collect documents and information, attend depositions or court trials with lawyers, and complete other tasks. Often, litigation support professionals must juggle multiple projects under tight deadlines. Most work at least full time, with some working more than forty hours per week when a deadline or trial date approaches.

Earnings

According to a survey by Salary.com, as of June 2017, the median annual pay for litigation support professionals was $83,855. In 2017 wages ranged from less than $55,339 to more than $105,745 for the highest-paid professionals.

Opportunities for Advancement

Entry-level professionals in this field often start as document coders or litigation support analysts. As they gain experience, litigation support professionals generally have the opportunity to take on more complex projects. They may be promoted to project manager positions, supervising a team of litigation support analysts and coders working on a large case. In larger organizations, they may advance to become a firm-wide litigation support manager or director. These senior professionals are responsible for the management of litigation support services and technologies across the entire firm or corporation.

Experienced litigation support professionals who demonstrate a record of excellent performance are more likely to be promoted. Earning professional certifications or a master's degree in computer science or a law degree can also improve a person's opportunities to advance.

What Is the Future Outlook for Litigation Support Professionals?

The job outlook for litigation support professionals is good. According to the BLS, computer occupations in the legal industry, which include litigation support professionals, are projected to grow 8 percent through 2022.

The extensive growth of electronically stored information has increased the complexity of litigation and discovery processes, a trend that is expected to continue. As such, litigation support professionals will be needed to organize, access, and protect this data. Those who have extensive work experience and are up-to-date on the latest technologies will have the best prospects for landing a job in this field.

Find Out More

Association of Legal Professionals
8159 E. Forty-First St.
Tulsa, OK 74145
website: www.nals.org

The Association of Legal Professionals is an organization for all professionals who support the legal industry, including litigation support professionals. Its website offers resources, a career center, a forum, and information about events, certification, and education.

International Legal Technology Association (ILTA)
9701 Brodie Ln., Suite 200
Austin, TX 78748
website: www.iltanet.org

The ILTA is an international membership organization that offers educational programming, publications, and knowledge-sharing communities to improve the use of technology in the legal profession.

Litigation Support Today
website: www.litsupporttoday.com

Litigation Support Today is an online magazine with information for litigation support professionals, including current and past issues of the magazine, a job board, industry news, events, and other resources.

Court Reporter

Court reporters create an official record of legal proceedings. They create word-for-word written transcripts of trials, depositions, hearings, and other legal proceedings that take place in federal, state, and municipal courts. They also create transcripts of everything said by lawyers and judges during meetings in the judge's chambers. They provide a complete and accurate record of these proceedings for later use by attorneys, judges, and others. Court reporters may also be called on to create a written transcript of depositions or meetings at attorney offices or other locations. Some court reporters also create transcripts for government proceedings such as legislative meetings and sessions in federal, state, or municipal government offices.

Most people speak between 150 and 250 words a minute, and court reporters must capture word for word every utterance during a court or other proceeding. This includes the statements and questions of lawyers and judges, as well as the testimony of every person called to the witness stand. To do this, they use specialized equipment, such as

At a Glance

Court Reporter

Minimum Educational Requirements
High school diploma or equivalent

Personal Qualities
Strong listening, writing, and organizational skills; concentration; attention to detail

Certification and Licensing
Required by some states

Working Conditions
Courthouses, law offices, and government offices

Salary Range
Median pay of $51,320 in 2016

Number of Jobs
As of 2014, about 20,800

Future Job Outlook
Projected growth of 2 percent through 2024

A court reporter creates the official record of a legal proceeding. Court reporters are responsible for creating word-for-word transcripts of trials, depositions, hearings, and other legal proceedings.

stenography machines, video and audio recording devices, and microphones to capture spoken dialogue. A stenography machine operates like a small keyboard. Instead of using letters, it creates words through key combinations, which enables court reporters to keep up with fast-paced courtroom dialogue. A computer program translates the key combinations into words and phrases to produce real-time, readable text.

Some court reporters use steno masks to transcribe speech. A steno mask is a handheld microphone that is built into a soundproof enclosure that fits over the court reporter's mouth. To use a steno mask, court reporters speak directly into the covered microphone, verbally narrating and recording the dialogue, gestures, and actions in the courtroom as they occur. The soundproof enclosure prevents others in the room from hearing what the court reporter is saying. Voice-recognition software converts the recording into a transcript that the court reporter reviews for accuracy and completeness.

Some court reporters use digital recorders to create an audio or video record of a proceeding. They take notes to identify speakers and give context for the recordings. They may also use the recording to create a written transcript.

After the proceeding is over, court reporters often work with a scopist to review the notes and recordings they have taken and create a written transcript. Scopists use specialized software to translate the transcript from the stenotype or steno mask into written English. They make sure all speakers' names are correct and edit the written transcript for any errors or misspellings. Then the court reporter proofreads the written transcript for final approval. The completed and approved transcript and any related recordings are given to the court, lawyers, and other parties involved in the proceeding. Court reporters also index and catalog exhibits used during legal proceedings. Their official record of the proceedings allows users to search for information contained in the transcript.

Cassandra Caldarella is a court reporter in the Orange County Superior Court in California. She explained why she loves being a court reporter in a 2015 interview posted on the Lifehacker website:

> The most enjoyable part of the job is being introduced to a vast and endless amount of information and always something new every day. I love meeting new people every day, whether it be attorneys, judges, clerks, bailiffs, other reporters, [or] expert witnesses. I get to be in the middle of all the action, hear the stuff nobody else gets to hear in chambers, and hear all types of stories for a living.

Caldarella is proud to provide a valuable service for people in court. "I am there at a very difficult and stressful time in people's lives. It's nice to know that people depend on me and that I'm helping them by providing them with an accurate record of their proceedings," she said.

How Do You Become a Court Reporter?

Education

Most court reporters have at least a high school diploma. In addition, many students enroll in formal court reporting programs at community colleges or technical institutes, where they can earn either a certificate or an associate's degree in court reporting. These programs can take two to five years to complete.

In a court reporting program, students will take courses in English grammar and phonetics, legal procedures, and legal terminology. They will also practice preparing transcripts and work on developing their speed and accuracy. Some training programs offer students the opportunity to learn how to use different transcription technology, such as stenotype machines or steno masks.

After earning a court reporting certificate or associate's degree, court reporters also complete a few weeks of on-the-job training. During this training, they practice specific skills. They might also spend time learning medical and technical terminology that is likely to come up in court proceedings.

Certification and Licensing

Many states require court reporters to be licensed by a state or certified by a professional association. Licensing requirements vary by state and court reporting method but generally involve passing a written test. Most court reporting training programs prepare students for state license tests.

In addition, several professional associations offer voluntary certifications for court reporters. The National Court Reporters Association offers certifications for court reporters, including the Registered Professional Reporter certification. Currently, twenty-two states accept this certification instead of a state certification or license test. The American Association of Electronic Reporters and Transcribers offers the Certified Electronic Reporter and Certified Electronic Transcriber certifications, while the National Verbatim Reporters Association offers certification for voice reporters who use steno masks. To earn these certifications, candidates typically must pass a written test and a skills test in which they must type, record, or transcribe a minimum number of words per minute with a high degree of accuracy. While these certifications are not required, earning them can give a job candidate an advantage.

Internships

Many schools that offer court reporting programs or certificates have a requirement that each student must participate in an internship to complete the program. Students often sit with court reporters while they work and follow them throughout the day so they can see first-hand what the job entails. They can see how intense the job can be, especially when court proceedings get heated. "When I did my internship hours I ended up taking part in a riveting murder trial; it was such great experience and really allowed me to see the exciting nature of the job itself, as well as how important it really is," said court reporter Taylor Bellais in a 2016 article posted on the Bryan University website.

Skills and Personality

Far and away the most important characteristic for a court reporter is being a good listener. Part of being a good listener is the ability to stay focused on the person who is speaking without letting any distractions get in the way. Courthouses are busy places, and even within a courtroom people may come and go. The court reporter must block out all of that activity to make sure he or she gets an accurate record of what is being said and what transpires. A lapse in concentration may cause a court reporter to miss a word or gesture that needs to be in the transcript.

Attention to detail is also critical for success. Court reporters must be able to produce accurate and error-free transcripts that serve as official legal records. For this same reason, they must have a strong command of grammar, spelling, and vocabulary. They must also handle information from a legal proceeding with integrity and make sure it is kept confidential.

Organization is also critical. "The most important thing in court reporting is to stay organized," Caldarella said. "We often juggle multiple deadlines for transcripts and we have to stay extremely organized in order to not miss a deadline. We've got to manage work that's out to scopists and proofreaders. . . . Our profession is deadline driven and organization is crucial."

On the Job

Employers

Most court reporters work in a court or legislative setting. According to the Bureau of Labor Statistics (BLS), there were approximately 20,800 court reporters working in the United States in 2014. While most court reporters work for municipal, state, or federal governments, some work as freelancers for law firms or corporations that want to obtain their own transcripts of court proceedings.

Working Conditions

Court reporters who work in courthouses typically work full time. Many travel to various courthouses or offices. During a proceeding, court reporters may work more than forty hours a week to ensure the transcript is ready on time. The job can be stressful when the reporter is trying to capture each word in a heated trial. Caldarella explained:

> It can be almost a 24/7 type of job. In court, I work 8:30 a.m. to 4:30 p.m. every day as an official, but I'm also an independent contractor. Transcripts are considered independent contractor work and must be done on my time. So after working seven hours per day in the courtroom, I must do transcripts on my time, which is during lunch, and in the mornings and evenings. I use a team of scopists and proofreaders to help me accomplish the high demand of producing daily transcripts when I'm in trial.

In some cases, court reporters may be able to work from a central office or from home, especially when preparing a transcript after a proceeding has ended.

Earnings

According to the BLS, the median annual earnings for court reporters was $51,320 as of May 2016. The top earners earned more than $95,990 while the lowest-paid 10 percent earned less than $26,610. The highest-paid court reporters worked for state governments and courts, earning a median annual salary of $54,040 as of May 2016.

Opportunities for Advancement

There are several ways for court reporters to advance their careers. One of the most common ways to advance is to move into positions in larger and more prestigious courts. For example, court reporters might start their careers by doing freelance depositions for law firms, then advance to a position at a municipal, state, or federal court. Some court reporters land prestigious assignments working for the US Senate or House of Representatives in Washington, DC.

Some court reporters choose to work as freelancers or form their own companies, providing their services on a work-for-hire basis. Some experienced court reporters choose to become teachers who train students in court reporting programs.

What Is the Future Outlook for Court Reporters?

According to the BLS's *Occupational Outlook Handbook*, court reporter positions are projected to grow 2 percent through 2024. Job growth in this field may be limited by the increased use of digital audio recording technology. Some states are evaluating the use of recording technologies to replace court reporters. Yet even in these cases, human court reporters will be needed to monitor recording equipment and produce transcripts. In addition, government budget constraints may also limit the number of court reporters hired by state and local governments.

Because there are a limited number of court reporter positions, competition for these jobs is expected to be strong. Candidates who have work experience and certifications will have the best prospects for landing a good job in this area.

Find Out More

American Association of Electronic Reporters and Transcribers (AAERT)
PO Box 9826
Wilmington, DE 19809
website: www.aaert.org

The AAERT provides education and certification for professionals engaged in digital reporting, transcribing, and associated roles.

National Court Reporters Association (NCRA)
12030 Sunrise Valley Dr., Suite 400
Reston, VA 20191
website: www.ncra.org

The NCRA, an educational and informational resource for people in the court reporting industry, provides certification programs for members. Its website has information about court reporting careers, education, certification and training, and industry news.

National Verbatim Reporters Association (NVRA)
629 N. Main St.
Hattiesburg, MS 39401
website: www.nvra.org

Founded in 1967, the NVRA is a national professional organization dedicated to the practice of voice writing (e.g., use of a steno mask). It offers information about certification, conferences, newsletters, and more.

United States Court Reporters Association
8430 Gross Point Rd., Suite 115
Skokie, IL 60077
website: www.uscra.org

The United States Court Reporters Association is the national representative for the federal court reporting profession. Its website has information about training, certification, jobs, and industry news.

Jury Consultant

What Does a Jury Consultant Do?

During jury selection, jury consultant David Cannon studies prospective jurors in court. He looks at their clothing and their body language as they listen to and answer questions from lawyers and judges. "Do they look comfortable? How are they dressed? Is how they are dressed what I would expect in relation to the part of town they are from? What does this tell me about their socio economic status? What does this tell me about their satisfaction with life?" Cannon said in a 2015 article posted on the Life of the Law website. Behind the scenes, Cannon's team uses the Internet to build complex, specific profiles of everyone in the jury box. He described a particular law enforcement case in which a prospective juror "was saying 'I love police, can't get enough of them.'" But Cannon had a feeling this attitude was not genuine. "That was red flag number one," he said. "Red flag number two was a picture of her on Facebook flipping off a police car." Cannon told the lawyer who hired him to dismiss the woman from the jury. This is the sort of expertise lawyers want jury consultants to provide when their client faces a jury trial.

At a Glance

Jury Consultant

Minimum Educational Requirements
Bachelor's degree, although master's degree or PhD often preferred

Personal Qualities
Insight into human behavior and motivations, strong interpersonal and communication skills, excellent presentation skills

Working Conditions
Office environment, courtroom settings

Salary Range
From about $44,000 to more than $100,000 in 2016

Future Job Outlook
Expected to be strong

Many cases proceed through the courts with only a judge making decisions. Fewer than 5 percent of civil and criminal cases are heard by juries. In these cases, lawyers for both sides have a say in who sits on the jury. The process of selecting a jury is called voir dire. The lawyers hope to seat a jury that will be more sympathetic to their client. While many lawyers rely on their own methods and experience for jury selection, in some cases lawyers turn to jury consultants. Because of the expense, for the most part, these experts are used in very high-profile cases or cases involving large companies or wealthy individuals.

Jury consultants assist clients in three main ways. First, they frequently organize and run mock trials, in which lawyers practice presenting their case and arguments in front of a test jury. The mock trial can reveal juror attitudes and reactions to lawyers' presentations and demeanor, which can give valuable insight into what factors may influence jurors' verdict decisions. A mock trial also helps lawyers, witnesses, and clients get a sense of what to expect in court and from opposing counsel.

After a mock trial, jury consultants help lawyers with the jury selection process. They develop questions for lawyers to ask potential jurors during voir dire. They carefully analyze and watch potential jurors' verbal responses and body language to advise the lawyer about whether to retain or dismiss them. Behind the scenes, a jury consultant's team scours the Internet and other public sources to uncover information about potential jurors to help with the selection process. At trial, building a favorable jury may be the difference between success or defeat in court.

During the trial, jury consultants continue to watch and study jurors. On the basis of their analysis of the jurors' body language, consultants advise the legal team on how their arguments and tactics are being received by the jury. This information can help the legal team tweak its strategy and arguments to achieve a more favorable reaction from the jury.

Roy Futterman is a clinical psychologist, jury consultant, and director at trial consulting firm DOAR. In his job, he leads a team of consultants to develop trial strategies for clients, creates focus groups and mock trials, helps lawyers with witness preparation and jury selection, and provides other consultation throughout a trial. In a February 2017 interview posted on Law360, Futterman talked about one of his most memorable cases. That case involved working with a group of female pharmaceutical sales representatives who sued their company for gender discrimination. Futterman said:

> While preparing the representatives to testify, I saw that many of them had a similar issue that was getting in the way of them speaking from their hearts. They had been heavily trained in giving sales presentations and this blocked the viewers' access to the emotions behind their stories. I worked with each of them to drop the sales front and to speak more directly from their hearts, and worked with each of them and their attorneys on developing the stories within their direct examinations so that each had a narrative arc and each echoed broader case themes in the openings, closings and others' testimonies. The sales representatives were astute learners and were able to tell their emotional stories in direct and powerful fashion, one after the other.

How Do You Become a Jury Consultant?

Education

Most jury consultants have at least a bachelor's degree in psychology, behavioral sciences, sociology, political science, criminology, or other related field. Some employers require jury consultants to have an advanced degree, such as a master's degree or a PhD in psychology, behavioral sciences, or a related field. Many jury consultants are professional psychologists who specialize in forensic psychology, the study of psychology and how it relates to criminals and others in the justice system, and have extensive experience in studying human behavior. In addition, a law degree can also be helpful but is not required. "There are no specific requirements or qualifications to be a litigation consultant," said Brad Bradshaw, a principal at Bradshaw Litigation Consulting in Austin, Texas, in a January 2017 article posted on the

Psychology Today website. "Having an advanced degree makes it much easier to get started but, if you are good at what you do, people will hire you. For litigation consulting, and many other consulting fields, knowledge, experience and connections are much more important than advanced degrees."

Getting Experience

Internships are available for college students who are already pursuing advanced degrees. These programs provide work experience and valuable skills that will help individuals stand out to potential employers. Rachel York, a litigation consultant with Magna Legal Services, says that her internship experiences while earning her doctorate in legal psychology were invaluable. In an interview posted on the CBS Philly website, she explained:

> I interned as a research assistant and later worked as a consultant at a litigation consulting firm as a graduate student, so I was able to transition to the working world while finishing my degree. While I had a smooth experience, colleagues of mine that were not able to gain consulting experience through internships or part-time work during graduate school found the transition to the working world more difficult, as many firms are only willing to hire consultants with at least some prior experience.

Bradshaw recommends that students look for creative ways to get exposure to the career and the legal process. In the above-mentioned article posted on the *Psychology Today* website, he explained how he simply went to court and watched trials:

> As simple as it sounds, it's the best way to get a feel for the job and learn how the process works. It was also a guaranteed way of getting into the room with potential clients (i.e., attorneys). While at the courthouse I also got to know the jury coordinator, who is the person in charge of sending out each jury summons and then directing potential jurors to various courtrooms.

By connecting with the jury coordinator I was always just a phone call away from finding out if there are any interesting trials on the docket. Try to think of clever ways to get free experience (even if you are not actively participating) and access to future clientele.

Skills and Personality

Jury consultants must have keen insight into human behavior and decision making. The most important part of their job is to interpret, understand, and analyze human thoughts, feelings, and behaviors. They use these skills to predict how individual jurors will react to information and arguments presented during a trial and the thought processes jurors use to make a decision.

Advanced research and analytical skills are also critical. Jury consultants research juror backgrounds and analyze data such as demographic information and polls to evaluate how a potential juror's opinion may be affected by factors such as age, sex, and income level. Jury consultants also analyze qualitative data such as verbal comments or opinions from interviews or written surveys.

In addition, jury consultants spend much of their time working with others, including people of all different backgrounds; having strong interpersonal skills makes this easier. Highly developed verbal and written communication skills are critical. Jury consultants must be able to present their conclusions and ideas quickly to their clients.

On the Job

Employers and Working Conditions

While some jury consultants work directly for large law firms, many work for private consulting firms or as independent consultants. Clients hire jury consultants on a contract basis for specific projects.

Jury consultants split their time between their offices, client sites, and courtrooms. They spend a lot of time with clients, which can require frequent travel. In order to meet tight deadlines, jury consultants often work more than forty hours per week.

Some jury consultants are self-employed, which allows them to have more control over their schedule. They can decide how many projects to take on and what travel they are willing (or unwilling) to do. However, because they only earn money when working on a project, self-employed jury consultants must devote time to selling their services and expanding their client base.

Earnings

According to the Balance, a personal finance website, salaries for jury consultants vary significantly by experience level, employer, and location. In 2016, wages ranged from around $44,000 to more than $100,000 for the highest-paid consultants. Jury consultants who work for a consulting company or law firm usually receive a base salary, while consultants who are self-employed are paid either by the hour or by the project.

Opportunities for Advancement

Experienced jury consultants generally have the opportunity to take on more high-stakes, high-profile projects. Senior consultants may supervise a team of consultants who are working on a large project. They may also focus on getting new clients or selling new projects to existing clients. Some consultants who work for a consulting firm may advance to higher-level positions and may even become a partner in the firm and share in its profits. Other experienced consultants may leave a consulting company to work for themselves or start their own jury consulting company. Earning advanced degrees in psychology, behavioral sciences, or a related field can also improve a person's opportunities for advancement.

What Is the Future Outlook for Jury Consultants?

As long as there are trials, there will be a need for jury consultants. While jury consulting is a small career field, it has grown steadily in recent years. Over the years, jury consultant Jo-Ellan Dimitrius has seen the number of jury consultants rise significantly. "A multiplicity of people have entered the profession," she said in a 2015 article in the

ABA Journal. "Jury consultants are now part of the legal culture for civil, criminal and corporate cases."

Jury consultants are often well paid. This makes these positions highly desirable. Therefore, candidates face strong competition for open positions. Those who have an advanced degree and work experience or are good at selling projects and bringing in clients will have the best prospects for landing a job in the field.

Find Out More

American Bar Association (ABA)
321 N. Clark St.
Chicago, IL 60654
website: www.americanbar.org

Not just for lawyers, the ABA is a voluntary bar association for the legal industry. Its site has resources and information for those interested in legal careers.

American Psychological Association (APA)
750 First St. NE
Washington, DC 20002
website: www.apa.org

The APA is a leading scientific and professional organization representing psychology in the United States. It has information about a variety of psychology-related careers, including trial and jury consulting.

American Society of Trial Consultants
206 S. Sixth St.
Springfield, IL 62701
website: www.astcweb.org

The American Society of Trial Consultants is a professional organization for trial and litigation consultants. Its website has information about membership, education, and conferences of interest to jury consultants.

Interview with a Lawyer

Susan M. Mooney is a lawyer who owns her own law firm in Stoneham, Massachusetts. She practices several areas of law, including personal injury, probate and estate administration, estate planning, real estate, and professional malpractice law. She answered questions about her career by e-mail.

Q: Why did you become a lawyer?

A: I always had a passion for protecting the rights of those unjustly treated and I was really good at making arguments and winning and really good as a voice for others who needed assistance. I enjoyed the course work in college that was law related, such as social sciences, economics, political science and history. I was a math major initially who changed to a psychology major (turned out to be a good undergrad degree basis for a client based law practice later). After college I was more interested in having a family and raising three young children. . . . Once my 3 children were old enough to be in school I decided it was time to make a decision on the idea of a career as a lawyer. So with lots of support and encouragement from my husband, I took the entrance exam and applied and got accepted and off to law school I went and have never looked back.

Q: What type of law do you concentrate in, and why did you choose this specialty?

A: My present practice concentrates in the area of estate planning (Wills and Trusts) and Medicaid planning (for Elder and/or Disabled persons in need of benefits to pay for costs of their care at home in the community or a rehab facility or nursing home settings) and Probate of Estates of deceased persons, and Elder Law (in same areas of practice, estate and Medicaid planning and asset preservation) focused on needs of the elder client. While 80 to 90 percent of my current practice is in the foregoing areas, I also handle some other civil matters such as Personal Injury cases (representing victims of accidents) and real estate transactions, mostly representing Sellers of a home by an individual or an Estate.

I chose these areas of practice somewhat by practicing for years learning what you like and what you don't like about cases and clients. I find with elder law and estate planning cases most clients are happy and truly appreciative of their lawyer's work and while this area of practice always accounted for a percentage of my caseload, it has evolved as a growing and favorite area of my practice over the years because clients are truly appreciative of the service and the assistance and for the most part it is non-adversarial. It is also flexible for scheduling which is appealing to me at this stage of my thirty-year career.

Q: Can you describe your typical workday?

A: My typical workday is an eight- to ten-plus-hour day. . . . If I have Court appearances my day may start early for an 8:30 a.m. hearing in the morning and then to the office in the afternoon. I generally have two to three client appointments per day, but keep one office day a week appointment free for research, paperwork, phone conferences, etc. Client appointments involve planning meetings, signing meetings with witnesses for estate plan document signing, real estate closings, etc. I do make home visits to clients due to the elder population I serve so appointments may be on the road or in the office or in the office of another attorney.

Most client appointments run an average of one to two hours, and frequently longer. In between appointments, phone calls and emails and research consume most of my day. If I do not have Court scheduled matters, I generally go to the office a little later in the morning and seldom leave the office before 7 or 8 p.m. in the evening as after appointments many calls are returned. I frequently work from home earlier in the morning or in the late evening answering emails.

Q: What do you like most about your job?

A: Mostly I like servicing the clients and solving their problems for the best result for that individual. All clients have unique and specific needs that must be addressed to meet their set of circumstances. I do not believe in cookie cutter planning and therefore all clients receive a plan that is specific to their needs. Many clients have special needs and may be confused about the process or their rights. I enjoy the satisfaction of providing a service to them that makes them feel secure and comfortable with the outcome.

Q: What do you like least about your job?

A: What I truly like least is not law related at all, but is the administrative matters of managing a law office or any small business. I do not like the staffing and employment issues or non-law-related parts of running a business over twenty-eight years, either as the managing partner in a small firm of two to three lawyers, or currently a solo practitioner.

Q: What personal qualities do you find most valuable for this type of work?

A: Our ethical rules and oath require zealous representation of every client; this means hard work, long hours and most of all loving what you do for work. As far as qualities, I would say people skills are critical, integrity, honesty and commitment are primary qualities; creativity and intelligence are important; compassion, tenacity, stamina, and perseverance are very helpful.

Q: What advice do you have for students who might be interested in this career?

A: Study hard. You have to enjoy lots of reading and writing. Being prepared for law school involves critical thinking and logical reasoning skills, lots of reading and learning legal writing skills, after your undergraduate degree, so be prepared for lots of years of education. Spend some time sitting in on law school classes and maybe spend a few days shadowing different kinds of lawyers (keeping in mind there are many different kinds of lawyers and spending a day in a courtroom with a district attorney on a criminal case, or a judge with many kinds of civil or criminal cases, is very different than spending a day with an estate planning lawyer like me, or a tax attorney who may work for the IRS, or a corporate lawyer who represents large or small businesses, or a domestic attorney who represents divorce clients, or a law professor who has never had a client practice at all). . . . You have to be passionate about a career as a lawyer to be successful and happy.

Other Jobs in the Legal Profession

Accident reconstructionist
Broadcast captioner
Computer forensics professional
Conflicts analyst
Contract administrator
Court clerk
Court messenger
Court recorder
Courtroom deputy
Court runner
District attorney
Document coder
E-discovery professional
Evidence technician
Family law specialist
Forensic scientist
Judge
Law clerk

Law firm administrator
Law professor
Law school admissions officer
Law school dean
Legal career counselor
Legal executive assistant
Legal file clerk
Legal receptionist
Legal recruiter
Legal secretary
Legal videographer
Magistrate
Penologist
Private investigator
Real-time stenographer
Scopist
Social worker

Editor's note: The US Department of Labor's Bureau of Labor Statistics provides information about hundreds of occupations. The agency's *Occupational Outlook Handbook* describes what these jobs entail, the work environment, education and skill requirements, pay, future outlook, and more. The *Occupational Outlook Handbook* may be accessed online at www.bls.gov/ooh.

Index

About the Author

Carla Mooney is the author of many books for young adults and children. She lives in Pittsburgh, Pennsylvania, with her husband and three children.